Finding My Song

Alexis Kennedy

BookLeaf Publishing
India | USA | UK

Presentation by *BookLeaf Publishing*

Web: www.bookleafpub.com

E-mail: info@bookleafpub.com

ISBN: 9789358369649

First edition 2023

DEDICATION

To everyone who ever had to find your song
again

ACKNOWLEDGEMENT

To the Fantastic Five and Bubba- thank you.
To Ronelle and Dominique- thank you.

PREFACE

The book was written when I thought I lost everything. I left an abusive marriage and then suffered a stroke at a young age, losing my ability to read and write and sing. I enrolled in a poetry challenge to learn to write again and also to heal. I am every day getting closer to finding my song again.

The Day I Couldn't Sing

I woke up this morning and couldn't sing.

And not that usual "Mary had a little lamb, I'm glad it's another day, sing a lullaby" kind of song.

And I woke up and did not have another, "Thank you Lord for another day, Hallelujah, Jesus is risen type" song.

I woke up this morning and couldn't see. I woke up this morning and didn't have a melody in my heart.
I woke up this morning with no drums in my ears and with no percussion in my feet.
I woke up this morning and couldn't sing.

Some might say it was the stress of work and traffic and parenting and PTA and relationships, the pressures of life. I am not sure what caused the void where there once was a melody but I woke up this morning and I couldn't sing.

I woke up this morning and I couldn't sing. I woke up this morning and there was no rums-the-rums in my hips. There was no clapping of my hands and harmony to provoke. This is the morning I woke up and there was no melody and thus, no hope. I realized I had no hope and thus… no joy, that Christ-given joy.

The kind of joy that makes you keep on believing, the kind of joy that makes you feel like there's something better coming tomorrow. The kind of joy that makes you want to get out of bed, want to leap, want to dream. Where had it gone?

Somewhere in the midst of life,
Of coming and going,
somewhere in the midst of being sick and being whole, somewhere in the midst of, "Will it ever happen?" and "It's never gonna happen," the melody was lost. The pages of the stanzas of my heart were torn, broken.

So then what can we say to these things?

The journey is going to come with highs and lows, but if my heart is still pumping, there is still a sound left in me.
And if I listen just hard enough, just long enough, I catch the rhythm.

The journey is going to come with ebbs and
flows; but I will allow the waves to move me,
surround me, shift me, not drown me. And if I
listen hard enough, just long enough, every
experience creates a melody.

There will be times that the rain will humble my
umbrella but the rain will someday stop. Until
then, every droplet, or rather experience, every
trial I overcome, every triumph I obtain, will be
a part of my symphony.

And someday I will dream again. Someday I
will hope again and there I'll find my melody.
Oh yes, someday I will sing again.

Dear Single Mom

Shoutout to you Single Mom.

You, who shows up for the little one every day.
You, who shows up in every way, even when
you're tired. Even when you had to hit the
snooze button seven times. To you, we say,
"Thank you."
You, the one who hastily leaves her job to pick
up your kids from school when they're sick and
rubs their belly to make them feel better.

You have to be the one who chases away the
monsters under the bed and read the bedtime
story when you would rather be alone in your
bed.

You, the one who stays up with them when
they're having a bad dream; you who has to dry
every tear.
You patch up the boo-boos, find a way to get
them to take medicine even when they don't
want to, you cook and do the laundry.
You keep up with every schedule and
appointment, show up to baseball games in your
work clothes but at least you make it.

Thank you.

Shoutout to you single mom for all the time you wondered how you were gonna make it; you didn't give up and somehow you made it through.

Shoutout to you single mom for all the times you would cry yourself to sleep hoping your kids wouldn't hear. You, for making sure the tank had gas and making sure the refrigerator had food, even if there was none for yourself.

Shoutout to you single mom for watching your kids make cartwheels on the floor and show you all of their latest drawings when all you wanted to do was literally nothing at all but you never let them see it.

Shoutout to you single mom for all the time you didn't get a break, didn't get a rest, didn't get vacation and couldn't find a sitter, couldn't go on a date but you never let the kids see you down.

Thank you.
Shoutout to you for every practice, every rehearsal you fought traffic to chauffeur to them to.

Thank you even when you have a reason, a real good one too, to trash down their father, you chose silence.
Thank you for the comfort.
Thank you for your discipline.
Thank you for not giving up.
Thank you for not throwing in the towel.
Thank you for not giving up without a fight.
Thank you for your strength.
Thank you.

For every seed you sow to persevere, one day you will see the fruit. One day you will see your children rising up and standing up, becoming greater than you dreamed or imagined. Because they watched their mother rise up and keep standing. You kept standing when obstacles came your way. You kept standing when life made you want to tap out. You stood for them and kept standing.
You are strong. You are capable. You are enough.
You, single mom, with your two arms to protect that baby, to provide for that baby, to nurture that baby.
You did it.

Shoutout to you, Single mom.
To you we say, "Thank you."

FAITH (haiku)

Faith is a great test.
It pushes, pulls and makes you wait.
BUT it has rewards.

The Living Well (haiku)

I drank from a well.
And it left me complete and whole.
Now I thirst no more.

Abba, Father

Abba means Father.

In times of clarity and joy, I'll call out the name
ABBA with elation, with Hallelujah.

In times of absolute praise I'll call out the name
ABBA with adoration, an eruption from my
belly all the way to my lips, exclaiming His joy,
His goodness and how He never left me.

But then there are other times.

In times of frustration and anguish, the name
ABBA has a different ring to it.
In those moments, sometimes it's a cry of
helplessness, sometimes it's with tears streaming
down my face saying, "Do you see me? Are you
with me?"

Sometimes it's with vengeance in my voice
saying, "Are you going to pay them back for
what they did to me, ABBA Father?"

"Are you gonna remove this bitter cup from me,
ABBA Father?"

"ABBA Father, where are you?"

In these moments, I have to remember, I GET to remember, He is ABBA, **MY** father.

He is my father. My father who never leaves me. And won't forsake me. My father who sees everything I'm going through and is protecting me, guiding me, loving me, comforting me.

He is my Father.
If I'm in this season and he's chastening me, it's because He loves me and that He knows that this discipline will purge me of some things and push me into some things. He knows that this discipline won't last forever, He knows that this discipline will only make me better, wiser.

My ABBA, my Father who cares for me, my father who provides for me even when I don't know what I'm asking for, my Father.

My Father who wants me to walk in the royal blood that He's called me to. I am, after all, the daughter of the King. The daughter of the King of kings, my Father.
From the tribulation, there WILL be TRIUMPH!

He's never going to leave me here any longer
than is necessary to get glory out of my life.

He's never gonna leave me here any longer than
is necessary to show His works, his GOOD
WORKS in my life. To show that "all things
work together," works in my life.
That "goodness and mercy that follow me,"
works in my life.

He won't leave me here any longer to necessary
to show someone His face, or show someone
how much they need to know Him too.

After all, He isn't just my Father. He's their
father too. Abba. Father.
My father, who's unlike any earthly father I've
ever known, has a plan for me.

And so in times of hope, I'll praise Him.
In times of trial, I'll praise Him.
In times of joy, I'll praise him.
In times of warfare, I'll praise Him.
In times of peace, I'll praise Him.
In times of sorrow, all praise Him.
In times of victory, I'll praise Him.

My father who cares for me and won't leave me.
My father who provides for me.

My father who clothes me.
My father who protects me from the snares of
my enemy.
My father who loved me before I ever even
knew what love was. My Father who promised
me that he always will!

My ABBA, My father.

Marriage (haiku)

Marriage mirrored me.
Showed me ME and made me grow.
Then it mirrored God.

Your Own Drum

You weren't made to fit in boxes; you were born
to break out.
It doesn't matter if no one else feels the rhythm;
just live your joy out loud.
And march to the beat of your own drum.

Right, left, right, left.
Your beat, your drum.
You may be louder than other people or maybe
soft-spoken.
Your figure may have a few extra pounds, or
your skin may be "too dark" or "too light."
But you march to the beat of your own drum.

The way you speak, the way you think, the way
you draw, the way you write,
the way you sing, the way you dance—
March to the beat of your own drum
Right, left, your beat.
Right, left, your drum.

There is no one else like you and there never
will be.
You are the original, you are a new creation, a
genesis, like nothing ever seen before.

March of the drum of your drum.

You are INIMITABLE. You are unique.
One of a kind.
You may be the first in your family to do it.
You may be the first in the world to do it.
But you march, baby, and you march to the beat
of your drum.

You weren't made to fit in boxes; you were born
to break out.
It doesn't matter if no one else feels the rhythm;
just live your life out loud.
And march to the beat of your own drum.
You're the rhythm of your joy, the cadence of
what makes you YOU.

It doesn't matter if no one else feels the rhythm;
just live your life out loud.
And march to the beat of your own drum.

Well Done (Haiku)

Oh, to hear, Well Done.
Not, "You always got it right."
"But still, child, well done."

Faith, Hope and Love

Faith and hope and love.
They say love is greater.
When we as individuals focus on actually *being* love, the world will be a better place.
When we as individuals focus on giving love instead of just receiving, the world would be a better place.
A card, an offering, a good deed, a call.
LOVE.
This love language, that love language, all of the above.
LOVE.
Love is what makes us forgive without an apology.
Love is what makes us give, even when we need the blessing ourselves.
Love is what changes the hearts of men and makes them have hope and faith again.
We can do a lot with faith, believing in something bigger than ourselves for something greater than ourselves.
We can do a lot with hope, expecting the unthinkable and the unimaginable. But even that is for ourselves.

But love, given without any measure of merit,
given even without them deserving it,
love given tangibly to those who need it the
most,
love given without even knowing if you're gonna
get it back, if it will be reciprocated,
love is greater and love will change the world.

The greatest of these is love.

Season (haiku)

Life's cold can't break me.
After winter, there is spring!
It's just a season.

The Other Side of Through
(haiku)

Push, Crawl, Fight, Run, PRESS
to the other side of through.
Great things wait for you.

But I Learned....

You did not fail.
You got up wiser this time.
You knocked down 1,2,3 or 7 times;
all that matters is that you get up at 8.
You didn't fail; you learned.

You learned to choose a little differently, had to
choose a little better.
You learned what it means to have a boundary
and set it and keep it.
And about yourself, your interests, your
relationship with yourself, your relationship with
God and your relationship with others.
You didn't fail, you learned.

You learned that a goal without application,
practicality, timing, focus, productivity,
accountability and alignment, makes that goal
just a dream.

And more than that, you learned that even
though God does give grace, He wants you to be
a better steward over your life,
a good steward over your life, every choice at a
time.

As kids you get the life you're given.
As adults you get the life you choose.
And now you know how to choose well.
You are not your past. You are not your
mistakes.
So no you didn't fail, you learned.

Confetti

I live life in the key of confetti.
Filled with music, the melody of laughter, fun
and love,
And leaving a sprinkle of joy in every room and
heart I enter.
Your life is a song.
What key are you singing it in?

JOY

I don't have to look too far,
I don't have to wish so hard,
I don't have to wait too long,
I know joy is coming.

Midnight lasted longer than I thought it should.
Everyone was telling me that it would work for
my good.
That every tear I cried and every sleepless night
I would get through.

When I didn't understand,
God I reached out for your hand
And you reminded me
To trust beyond what I can see,
because you always have a plan

I don't have to look too far,
I don't have to wish so hard,
I don't have to wait too long,
I know joy is coming.

I'll call you Jireh for a reason;
You constantly provide everything I need
Whether I'm in or out of season.

Weeping endures for a night
but I know I will be alright
YOU PROVIDE THE MORNING LIGHT!
And I KNOW joy is coming!

1 Peter 5:8

Whew, there goes the voice of the enemy,
Doing what he does usually,
Walking about, prowling, roaring,
Telling me what I am not.

But I have a greater voice inside of me,
Telling me all the great things that I *can* be.
I'm God's sheep so the devil cannot get to me.
I remember, but maybe he forgot.
I am safe
I am loved
I am chosen
I am redeemed
I'm strong
I'm capable
I'm enough
And even when I'm not enough, I serve the one
who is

Oh dear lion, you should have devoured me last
season but I woke up and found God's strength.

And now I know who I am.
I know the greater one is on the inside of me,

I know I'm made in His image, and in this
season absolutely nothing can stop me.

Lead Me

I don't wanna be ahead of you.
I don't wanna be too slow and get too far behind.
I want to be e exactly where you tell me to
Your plans are better than my own;
Your timing is better than my own.
Where you lead me, I'll follow.
Where you guide me, I'll stand.
What you show me, I'll trust.
I'm staying in your hand.

Finish Strong

Never met a mountain I couldn't climb.
Never met a giant that I couldn't slay.
I'm built for this.
Pressure makes diamonds, that's what they say.
That's why I keep shining; that's why I don't
break.
Unstoppable. Unbreakable.
Undeniable. Uncrushable.

I'm stronger than I ever knew I was, and every
battle proves that more and more.
The giants get bigger, I get stronger.
I'm built for this.
I'm made for this.
I'll make it to the finish line and I'll finish strong.

To Cam

Dear Cam:
I've told you since you were born that you're amazing,
I've told you since you became a teenager that you are a prize.
I know sometimes we've been up and sometimes we've been down
Sometimes life gives us joy and sometimes a little crazy, but we made it!
Every single day I pray you never lose that sparkle of joy in your eyes.
I don't profess as a mother to have gotten everything right or anything right
But one thing that I know I pray every night that you always know who you are:
Loved by God, chosen by God.
That you always know you're beautiful and so deserving of real love
That you learn from our mistakes so you don't have to make them,
that you have a forgiving but WISE heart.
That you apply yourself and shoot for every single dream under the stars
That you know you can do anything and be anything

This world is yours!

I pray that you know you are valuable and
talented and such a great leader,
That you know that you're unstoppable.

I mean what I say when you get out of the car
every morning, That "you are amazing, that you
are loved that you can handle anything" and I
pray you always know that.
I believe in you. And I pray you always believe
in you too.

Go conquer the world!